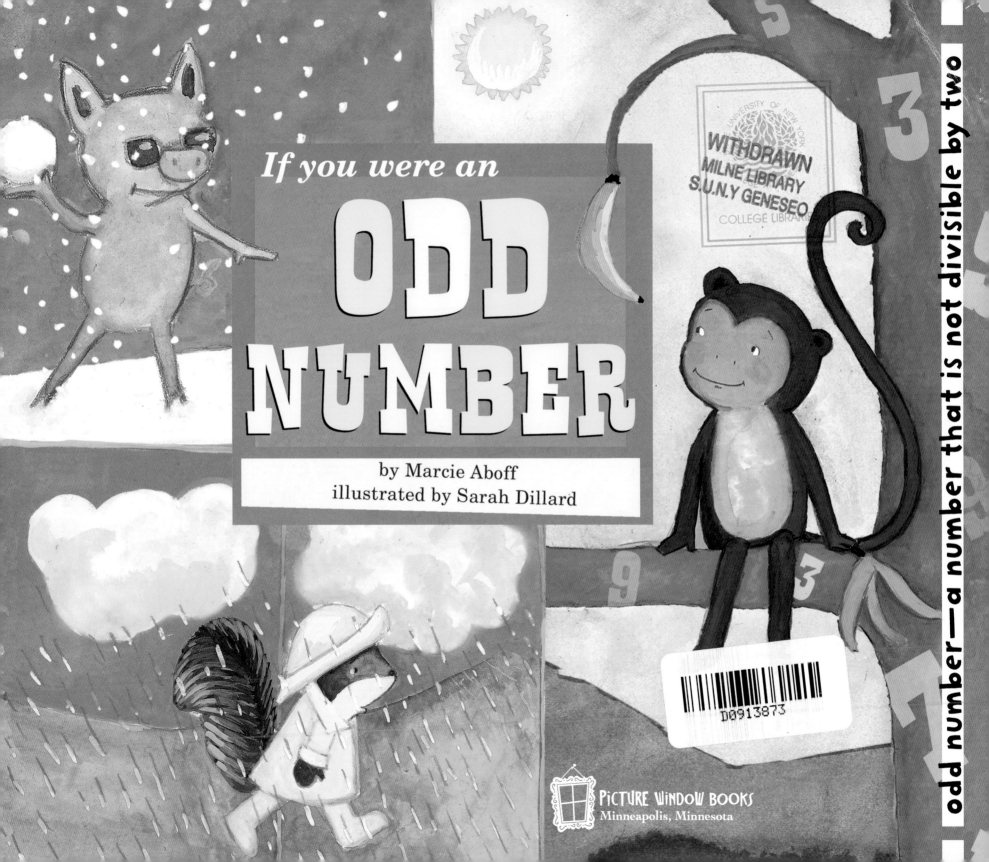

If you were an ODD NUMBER

by Marcie Aboff

illustrated by Sarah Dillard

PICTURE WINDOW BOOKS
Minneapolis, Minnesota

Editor: Christianne Jones
Designers: Nathan Gassman and Hilary Wacholz
Page Production: Melissa Kes
The illustrations in this book were created with acrylics.

Picture Window Books
151 Good Counsel Drive
P.O. Box 669
Mankato, MN 56002-0669
877-845-8392
www.picturewindowbooks.com

Printed in the United States of America.

All books published by Picture Window Books
are manufactured with paper containing at least
10 percent post-consumer waste.

Library of Congress Cataloging-in-Publication Data
Aboff, Marcie.
If you were an odd number / by Marcie Aboff ; illustrated by
Sarah Dillard.
p. cm. — (Math fun)
Includes index.
ISBN 978-1-4048-4793-4 (library binding)
ISBN 978-1-4048-4794-1 (paperback)
1. Numbers, Prime—Juvenile literature. I. Dillard, Sarah,
1961- ill. II. Title.
QA246.A36 2009
513.2—dc22
2008006455

Special thanks to our advisers for their expertise:

Stuart Farm, M.Ed., Mathematics Lecturer
University of North Dakota

Terry Flaherty, Ph.D., Professor of English
Minnesota State University, Mankato

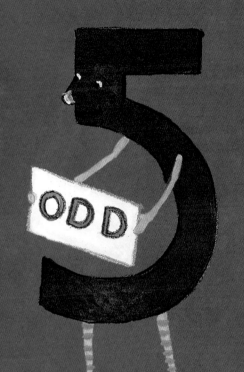

If you were an odd number...

... you could be the starting lineup.

The 5 basketball players scrambled down the court.

The 9 baseball players ran onto the field.

The 11 football players huddled by the end zone.

If you were an odd number, you would not be divisible by 2. There would always be a remainder of one left over.

The tree had 3 bananas. Two monkeys each ate 1 banana. One banana was left over. Three is an odd number.

Two mice had 7 pieces of cheese. Each mouse ate 3 pieces of cheese. One piece of cheese was left over. Seven is an odd number.

If you were an odd number, your last digit would be 1, 3, 5, 7, or 9.

Patrick guessed there were 253 jellybeans in the jar.

Paula guessed there were 459 jellybeans in the jar.

Patricia guessed there were 787 jellybeans in the jar.

Patsy guessed the right answer. There were 645 jellybeans in the jar!

If you were an odd number, you could count in groups of five. You could use tally marks to add things up quickly.

Mrs. Smith dressed in colorful clothes. She asked the students which of the 3 colors on her dress they liked best.

Blue got 5 votes. Yellow got 7 votes. And red got 13 votes.

If you were an odd number, you would be between two even numbers. You would be every other counting number on a number line, starting with 1.

13

If you were an odd number, you could add yourself to an even number and get an odd answer.

Jessie gathered 5 (odd) red apples and 6 (even) green apples. He had 11 (odd) apples in all.

But if you were an odd number and added yourself to another odd number, you would get an even answer.

Maggie gathered 7 (odd) green apples and 3 (odd) red apples. She had 10 (even) apples in all.

If you were an odd number, you could be the seven days of the week.

Monday, Tuesday, and Wednesday were rainy. It rained 3 days.

Thursday, Friday, and Saturday were snowy. It snowed 3 days.

day	Friday	Saturday	Sunday

Sunday was sunny. It was the 1 perfect day to throw snowballs!

If you were an odd number,
you could be a traffic sign.

All of the fish slowed down at the 3-sided yield sign that was posted near the 5-sided school zone sign.

If you were an odd number, you could light up the sky.

Seven lazy lobsters worked on their tans under 1 shining sun.

Five cool crabs relaxed under 1 glowing moon.

You would not mind being different ...

ODD

... if you were an odd number.

Sometimes it's cool to be odd. Find out how odd you are by answering the following questions. See how many odd numbers you get. Then ask your friends how odd they are.

1. How old are you?

2. What date is your birthday?

3. What is the last number in your telephone number?

4. What is the last number in your home address?

5. How many people are in your family?

Glossary

digit—a number between zero and nine

divisible—able to be separated into equal parts

even number—a number that is divisible by two

odd number—a number that is not divisible by two

remainder—a leftover number

tally marks—marks that show the number of items; usually grouped by five

To Learn More

More Books to Read

Fisher, Doris, and Dani Sneed. *One Odd Day.* Mount Pleasant, S.C.: Sylvan Dell Publishing, 2006.

Hall, Pamela. *The Odds Get Even!: The Day the Odd Numbers Went on Strike.* Los Angeles: Pigg Toes Press, 2003.

Lewis, J. Patrick. *Arithme-Tickle: An Even Number of Odd Riddle-Rhymes.* San Diego: Harcourt, Inc., 2002.

On the Web

FactHound offers a safe, fun way to find Web sites related to topics in this book. All of the sites on FactHound have been researched by our staff.

1. Visit *www.facthound.com*
2. Type in this special code: 1404847936
3. Click on the **FETCH IT** button.

Your trusty FactHound will fetch the best sites for you!

Index

Look for all of the books in the Math Fun series:

If You Were a Fraction

If You Were a Minus Sign

If You Were a Plus Sign

If You Were a Set

If You Were an Even Number

If You Were an Odd Number

24